# From Bird Poop to Wind

## How Seeds Get Around

### by Ellen Lawrence

**Consultants:**

**Suzy Gazlay, MA**
Recipient, Presidential Award for Excellence in Science Teaching

**Dr. Robin Wall Kimmerer**
Professor of Environmental and Forest Biology
SUNY College of Environmental Science and Forestry, Syracuse, New York

**Kimberly Brenneman, PhD**
National Institute for Early Education Research, Rutgers University
New Brunswick, New Jersey

**BEARPORT**
PUBLISHING

New York, New York

**Credits**

Cover, © Mike Martin/Ozark Nature Gallery; 3L, © Dariusz Majgier/Shutterstock; 3TR, © Shebeko/Shutterstock; 3BR, © Madlen/Shutterstock; 4, © Pam Penick; 5, © Bill Draker/Imagebroker/FLPA; 6BL, © Steve Hurst/ USDA; 6BR, © Alex Staroseltsev/Shutterstock; 7, © Rolf Nussbaumer Photography/Alamy and © Inga Nielsen/ Shutterstock; 8, © Sofiaworld/Shutterstock; 9TR, © Chris & Tilde Stuart/FLPA; 9MR, © Wikipedia Creative Commons; 9BL, © Chris & Tilde Stuart/FLPA; 9BR, © AfriPics.com/Alamy; 10L, © Shebeko/Shutterstock; 10R, © Lori Labrecque/Shutterstock; 11, © Dudarev Mikhail/Shutterstock; 12R, © Wikipedia Creative Commons; 12L, © Igor Grochev/Shutterstock; 13, © Scott Camazine/Alamy; 14L, © Teze/Shutterstock; 14R, © Mihai Simonia; 15TL, © Anette Linnea Rasmussen/Shutterstock; 15BM, © Dariusz Majgier/Shutterstock; 15BR, © Krasowit/ Shutterstock; 16, © Warakorn/Shutterstock; 17L, © Iakov Kalinin/Shutterstock; 17TR, © sunsetman/Shutterstock; 17BR, © OlegD/Shutterstock; 18, © Nigel Cattlin/FLPA; 19, © Avi ben zaken; 20, © Le Do/Shutterstock; 21, © Sergiy Bykhunenko/iStock Photo; 22TL, © Tungphoto/Shutterstock and © Ivonne Wierink/Shutterstock; 22TR, © SMcAfoos/Shutterstock and © TFoxFoto/Shutterstock; 22BL, © Tischenko Irina/Shutterstock; 22BM, © LianeM/ Shutterstock and © Valentyn Volkov/Shutterstock; 22BR, © Jerry Friedman/Wikipedia Creative Commons; 23TL, © Paul Maguire/Shutterstock; 23TR, © Davydova Svetlana/Shutterstock; 23BL, © Krasowit/Shutterstock; 23BR, © Steve Hurst/USDA.

Publisher: Kenn Goin
Editorial Director: Adam Siegel
Creative Director: Spencer Brinker
Design: Elaine Wilkinson
Photo Researcher: Ruby Tuesday Books Ltd


*Library of Congress Cataloging–in-Publication Data*

Lawrence, Ellen, 1967–
  From bird poop to wind : how seeds get around / by Ellen Lawrence.
      p. cm. — (Plant-ology)
  Includes bibliographical references and index.
  ISBN 978-1-61772-585-2 (library binding) — ISBN 1-61772-585-4 (library binding)
  1. Seeds—Dispersal—Juvenile literature. 2. Seeds—Ecology—Juvenile literature. 3. Germination. I. Title.
QK929.L376 2013
575.6'8—dc23
                              2012016963

For more information, write to Bearport Publishing Company, Inc., 45 West 21st Street, Suite 3B, New York, New York 10010. Printed in the United States of America.

10 9 8 7 6 5 4 3 2 1

# Contents

# A Fruity Meal

A hungry cardinal is eating **berries** from a holly bush.

It is eating the **seeds** inside the berries, too.

After its meal, the cardinal flies off to look for more food.

The bird doesn't know it, but now it has an important job to do.

Soon it will help the holly bush make new plants!

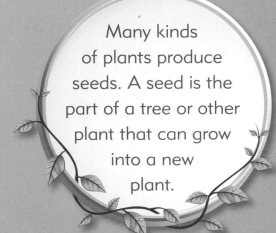

Many kinds of plants produce seeds. A seed is the part of a tree or other plant that can grow into a new plant.

holly bush

cardinal

holly berries

How do you think the cardinal will help the holly bush make new plants?

5

# Cardinal Poop

As the cardinal flies through a forest—splat!

A blob of cardinal poop falls to the ground.

Inside the poop are seeds from the holly berries.

The seeds have passed through the bird's body and landed in a place where they can grow.

The bird has helped the holly bush by spreading its seeds to a new home!

Flowering plants grow their seeds inside fruits, which help protect the seeds. Some fruits, such as berries or apples, are soft. Others, such as acorns or coconuts, are hard.

a close-up picture of holly seeds

apple seed

Why do you think it's important for a plant's seeds to be spread to new places?

# What Do Seedlings Need?

Many new plants, or seedlings, can't grow if they are too close to their parent plant.

The bigger plant may block out the sunlight a seedling needs to live.

Also, there may not be enough water and **nutrients** in the soil for both plants.

Then the little plant will die.

Plants can't move around and drop their seeds in new places.

Luckily, some animals eat seeds and then poop them out far from the parent plant.

seedling

African elephants eat the fruit and seeds of the marula tree. They may walk many miles and then drop the tree's seeds to the ground in their poop.

elephant shaking marula tree to get fruit

elephant poop

marula fruit

marula seeds

marula seedlings growing in dry poop

# Animals Plant Seeds!

Animals don't just spread seeds in their poop—
they move them around in other ways, too.

For example, squirrels eat acorns, which
contain the seeds of oak trees.

They collect acorns from under oak trees and
then bury them in new places.

In winter, when there is not much food,
squirrels dig up and eat the acorns.

Any acorns the squirrels don't dig up may
grow into new oak trees, far from their
parent tree!

squirrel

acorns

oak tree in the fall

Animals spread seeds in their poop and by burying them in new places. In what other way might an animal move seeds around?

Some kinds of ants eat seeds. They collect seeds from plants and store them in their underground nests. Some seeds don't get eaten and grow into new plants.

11

# Hitching a Ride

Some seeds move away from their parent plant by getting stuck on an animal's body.

Burdock plant seeds grow together in balls called burrs.

Each seed has a little hook on the end.

When an animal brushes past the burdock, the burrs hook onto the animal's fur or wool.

Then the seeds hitch a ride to a new place!

When people walk through fields or forests, they often get small, spiky pieces of plants stuck to their clothes. These sticky plant pieces are seeds on their way to a new place.

a burdock burr

hook

burdock flower

burr

dog

burrs

Seeds aren't just spread by animals. What type of weather could help seeds move to a new place?

# Blowing in the Wind

Some seeds are blown to new places by the wind.

The longer a seed stays up in the air, the further it can be carried by the wind.

A dandelion seed has a tiny fluffy parachute that helps it float in the air.

Maple tree seeds have wings that make them spin in the air like tiny helicopters.

This spinning movement helps the seeds stay up in the air for as long as possible.

parachute

dandelion

wing

maple tree seed

A poppy's seeds are inside a **seedpod** that has lots of tiny holes. When the wind blows the seedpod from side to side, the seeds scatter through the holes like pepper from a pepper shaker.

hole

poppy seeds

dandelion seed

poppy seedpod

# Floating to a New Home

The seeds of some plants that grow near water may float to a new home.

Coconut palm trees often grow on beaches next to the ocean.

Each palm tree seed grows inside a fruit called a coconut.

Some coconuts fall from their tree and float out to sea.

They may be washed up on beaches miles from their parent plant.

On the new beaches, the coconuts may grow into new palm trees.

coconuts

outer skin
of coconut

seed hole

seed shell

Inside the hard outer skin of a coconut there is a tough, hairy shell that surrounds the seed. The shell has three holes. The new palm tree grows out of one of these holes.

new palm tree

coconut palm tree

# High-Speed Seeds

Some plants spread their seeds by shooting them a long distance at high speed!

Squirting cucumber plants are in the same plant family as zucchini and cucumbers that people eat.

Hairy, green fruits grow on the plant.

Each fruit fills up with seeds and juice and gets fatter and fatter.

Finally, the fruit explodes, and the seeds are blasted far from the parent plant.

fruit

squirting cucumber plant

When a squirting cucumber's seeds are shot from the plant, they travel at about 60 miles per hour (97 kph). That's as fast as a car speeding along a highway!

seeds blasting from fruit

fruit

# Seeds on the Move

Plants spread their seeds with the help of wind and water.

Animals carry seeds to new places on their fur and in their stomachs!

Plants are not able to move around.

However, they have plenty of ways to move their seeds to new places!

Sometimes people help plants grow in new places. They buy seeds from a garden center and plant them or scatter them in their gardens and yards.

# Science Lab

## Be a Seed Detective

Plants get help spreading their seeds from the wind, water, animals, and even people.

Many seeds get help in more than one way.

Look at the pictures of plants and seeds on this page.

How do you think these seeds might move to new places?

Write down your ideas and compare them to the answers on page 24.

water lily seedpod

cattail plant seeds

apple tree seeds

hazel tree seeds

This part is the seed.

The seeds are in this pod.

devil's claw plant seeds

# Science Words

**berries** (BEHR-eez) small fruits, such as blueberries, blackberries, and holly berries, that contain a seed or seeds

**nutrients** (NOO-tree-uhnts) substances that plants get from the soil, such as nitrogen, which a plant needs to grow leaves and be healthy

**seedpod** (SEED-pod) a protective case that contains a plant's seeds

**seeds** (SEEDZ) small parts of a plant that can grow into new plants

23

# Index

# Read More

Spilsbury, Louise and Richard. *How Do Plants Grow? (World of Plants)*. Chicago: Heinemann (2006).

Weakland, Mark. *Seeds Go, Seeds Grow (A+ Books: Science Starts)*. Mankato, MN: Capstone (2011).

Weiss, Ellen. *From Seed to Dandelion (Scholastic News Nonfiction Readers: How Things Grow)*. New York: Scholastic (2008).

# Learn More Online

To learn more about seeds, visit
**www.bearportpublishing.com/Plant-ology**

# About the Author

Ellen Lawrence lives in the United Kingdom. Her favorite books to write are those about nature and animals. In fact, the first book Ellen bought for herself, when she was six years old, was the story of a gorilla named Patty Cake that was born in New York's Central Park Zoo.

# Answers

**Page 22:** Be a Seed Detective

Apple tree seeds are eaten by birds and other animals.

Water lily seeds float to new places in water.

Cattail plants have fluffy seeds that blow away in the wind or float in water.

Hazel tree seeds are sometimes collected and buried by small animals such as squirrels and chipmunks.

Devil's claw seedpods hook onto animals and people and get a ride to new places.